THE
BIBLE STUDY
BLUEPRINT

AN ESSENTIAL GUIDE FOR STUDYING GOD'S WORD

HAMP LEE III

(com)mission™
PUBLISHING

PRATTVILLE, AL

CONTENTS

INTRODUCTION

The Bible is the most important book ever written. It reveals the beauty of everything good God created and the depravity which came into the world through sin. And through God's love and mercy, we find salvation and eternal life through His son.

As God loved the world and gave His only begotten Son,[1] I believe understanding God's message is essential for learning about God, living for God, and preparing to spend an eternity with Him. And this is my reason for writing *The Bible Study Blueprint: An Essential Guide for Studying God's Word*.

The purpose of *The Bible Study Blueprint* is to provide you with tools and resources to study and understand God's word. This book begins with the history of the creation of the Bible we have today and the purpose of multiple Bible versions in the marketplace. I'll continue with a summary of the

---

[1] John 3:16.

Bible as well as outlining its significant sections and divisions. In the remaining chapters, I'll provide four methods to study passages of scripture: passage study, word study, outline study, and personal profile study.

Give diligence to present yourself approved by God, a workman who doesn't need to be ashamed, properly handling the Word of Truth.[2]

---

[2] 2 Timothy 2:15.

WHY STUDY
THE BIBLE?

Every Scripture is God-breathed and profitable for teaching, for reproof, for correction, and for instruction in righteousness, that each person who belongs to God may be complete, thoroughly equipped for every good work.[3]

A few decades after Jesus' death, a man named Paul wrote the message above in a second letter to his young follower, Timothy. Paul, who was called by God to share the Gospel with non-Jews (Gentiles), was now in prison for preaching about Jesus. This letter, which is named 2nd Timothy (or 2 Timothy), was the last recorded letter to be included in the Bible.

Paul tells Timothy the purpose of scripture and what it's profitable for in the verses above. First, he lets Timothy know that every scripture is God-breathed.

---

[3] 2 Timothy 3:16–17.

What this means is that God inspires every scripture. Though different people wrote different parts of the Bible, it was ultimately God who divinely led them to write.

If you look back to 2 Timothy 3:16–17, every scripture is also profitable (helpful, serviceable, advantageous, yielding or bringing profit or gain) for:

1. teaching—instruction, doctrine, or learning,

2. reproof—proof, conviction, evidence,

3. correction—straightening up again...rectification (reformation), chastisement, nurturing in living a righteous Christian life,

4. instruction in righteousness—tutorage, education or training; by implication, disciplinary, with a purity of heart and uprightness of life,

The benefit of every scripture is that each person who belongs to God experiences two things:

1. Completion. The word complete in this verse is defined as perfect. This is having all the required or desirable elements, qualities, or characteristics; free from any flaw or defect in condition or quality.

2. Equipping. Each person who belongs to God is thoroughly furnished for every beneficial and valuable work. *Think about this for a moment.* There is no good work that you wouldn't accomplish because God's word perfected you through teaching, reproof, correction, and instruction in righteousness.

EXEGESIS

Exegesis is an explanation or interpretation intended to explain or illustrate a subject. Outside of seminaries and other Christian academic settings, discussions on *exegesis*—what it is and how it can be used—is mostly silent. But I believe disciples of Christ should strive to understand how a proper exegesis can benefit them within personal and community Bible studies.

As the Bible spans thousands of years outside of your cultural and societal norms, a proper exegesis can help you accurately interpret and explain God's word as it was first written to its original audience. As you understand the scriptures you read and study within that context, you'll have the information available to assess what the scriptures say as a direct application, a principle to follow, or information of a historical, yet supernatural event.

When writing to Timothy, Paul also mentioned that he should *give diligence to present himself approved by God, a workman who doesn't need to be ashamed, properly handling the Word of Truth.*[4] As we strive to be such workmen, it's important to conduct a proper exegesis by *asking questions* of the scriptures we study. This is a diligent work that's accomplished through the exploration of several questions, such as:

Who wrote the book?

Why did the writer write the book?

Who was the writer's original audience?

Were there any cultural, political, or social situations that motivated the writer's message?

What was the overall theme of the book?

What personal applications, if any, are there?

The last question about personal application is often the question that most answers first. And after answering, will leave the others unanswered. But for a proper understanding of the biblical text, we must seek to answer these questions. This requires proper exegesis.

---

[4] 2 Timothy 2:15.

OVERVIEW
OF THE BIBLE

The Bible is comprised of sixty-six separate books. *You can think of these separate books like chapters.* The books are divided into the Old and New Testament, *like sections.* The Old Testament contains thirty-nine books and the New Testament, twenty-seven books. Each book shares a particular message of God's purpose and will. Some books are for specific people, while others are for all people to follow and obey.

The Old and New Testaments represent separate covenants *or contracts* God established with specific groups of people. The first covenant was ratified with the people of Israel thousands of years ago. Much of this covenant's history and commands serve as a historical reference of God's election and purpose in representing Himself through one specific group of people.

The New Testament is the history of God's covenant for all people worldwide, including the people of Israel. Like the Old Testament, the New Testament tells the history of the new covenant established through God's Son, Jesus.

The Old Testament was primarily written in Hebrew and the New Testament in Greek. There are sections in both the Old and New Testaments that were written in Aramaic.[5]

Together, the Old and New Testaments share one story of God's love for His creation and what He does to bring us back to Himself forever.

Canon

The *International Study Bible Encyclopedia* defines "canon" as a Greek word meaning a reed, measuring rod, norm, or rule.[6] And as such, *canon* came to be known as a rule of faith, a catalog or list of selected books that would be identified as divinely inspired. The selection of the Old and New Testaments didn't come from a church authority or person. Just as the

[5] Evans, Craig A., 1999, "What Bible Version did Jesus Read?" *Christianity Today*, Apr 26, 1998, https://search.proquest.com/docview/211917466?accountid=43702.

[6] "Canon of the Old Testament, I - International Standard Bible Encyclopedia," Blue Letter Bible, Last Modified 5 May, 2003, https://www.blueletterbible.org/search/Dictionary/viewTopic.cfm.

Holy Spirit moved upon the writers to inspire the books we have, we believe the same occurred for the canonization of both testaments.[7]

Old Testament

Then he said to them, "These are my words that I spoke to you while I was still with you, that everything written about me in the Law of Moses and the Prophets and the Psalms must be fulfilled."[8]

Jesus identified the Old Testament canon as the Law of Moses, the Prophets, and the Psalms. Though there is no scholarly consensus for the canonization of the Hebrew Bible, its formation, called the Tanakh, was completed around 450 B.C. and has remained unchanged throughout the ages.[9]

The Tanakh encompasses twenty-four books and its subdivisions are an acronym of Tanakh:

Torah (Law)—Teaching, the five books of Moses (Genesis, Exodus, Leviticus, Numbers, and Deuteronomy). The Torah is also called the

---

[7] 2 Peter 1:21.

[8] Luke 24:44

[9] Khoo, Jeffrey, Canon, Texts, and Words: Lost and Found or Preserved and Identified?, Far Eastern Bible College, Accessed February 5, 2020, https://www.febc.edu.sg/v15/article/def_canon_texts_words.

Pentateuch.[10] The Pentateuch, which means five vessels or containers, are the first five books of the Bible. They describe the creation of the earth and man and the entry of sin in man and the world. They also outline God's redemptive plan from one man through the nation of Israel and the covenant and laws God established with them.

Nevi'im (spokespersons or Prophets)—Former prophets: Joshua, Judges, Samuel, and Kings. These books relate to Israel's history from their entry into their promised land, rise to prominence as a nation, division into two kingdoms (Israel and Judah), and their exile to Babylon.[11]

Latter prophets: Isaiah, Jeremiah, Ezekiel, and the Book of the Twelve (Hosea, Joel, Amos, Obadiah, Jonah, Micah, Nahum Habakkuk, Zephaniah, Haggai, Zechariah, and Malachi). The latter prophets provide an assessment of Israel's and Judah's punishment and their restoration toward a holy ideal.[12]

---

[10] Mann, Thomas W., *The Book of the Torah,* Wipf and Stock Publishers, 2013, vii.

[11] Sweeney, Marvin A., *The Prophetic Literature: Interpreting Biblical Texts Series*, Abingdon Press, Nashville: 2010, 19.

[12] Ibid.

Ketuvim—Writings (Poetic books): Psalms, Proverbs, and Job; (Scrolls or Megillot): Song of Solomon, Ruth, Lamentations, Ecclesiastes, and Esther; (Prophecy): Daniel; and (History): Ezra, Nehemiah, and 1 and 2 Chronicles. The Ketuvim represents a miscellaneous collection of books before the Babylonian Exile in the early 6th century B.C. to the middle of the 2nd century B.C.[13] These literary works encompass sacred and erotic poetry, practical philosophy or wisdom, history, short stories, personal narratives, apocalyptic literature, and more.[14] *Studying the Bible: The Tanakh and Early Christian Writings* sees the Ketuvim as a "meditative reflection" of Jewish life and an "attempt to capture and preserve the ancient traditions, history, customs, and beliefs of the Israelites" following their return from exile.[15]

The twenty-four books of the Tanakh encompass the thirty-nine books of our Protestant Old Testament.[16]

---

[13] *Britannica Academic*, s.v. "Ketuvim," accessed July 11, 2019, https://academic-eb-com.eu1.proxy.openathens.net/levels/collegiate/article/Ketuvim/45206.

[14] Eiselein, Gregory, Anna Goins, and Naomi J. Wood, *Studying the Bible: The Tanakh and Early Christian Writing*s (Manhattan: New Prairie Press, 2019), 90.

[15] Ibid., 91.

[16] A Protestant is considered a member or follower of any of the Western Christian churches that are separate from the Roman Catholic Church and follow the principles of the Reformation, including the Baptist, Presbyterian, and Lutheran churches.

The Tanakh counts Samuel, Kings, Chronicles, Ezra, Nehemiah as one book, and the latter minor prophets as another.

Protestants, Orthodox Christians, and Roman Catholics each use different canons for their Old Testament writings. Though Protestant and Catholic canons differ on their inclusion of the Apocrypha in their Bibles, they each use the Hebrew Tanakh as their source scripture.[17] The Orthodox Christian canon uses the Greek version of the Old Testament, known as the Septuagint.[18]

New Testament

Much like the Old Testament, the creation of the New Testament Scriptures is not easy to follow

---

[17] Although the Jews and Protestants rejected the Apocrypha, the Roman Catholic Church, as well as some other Christian communities, considers it to be divinely authoritative. Consisting of twelve books, they were written between the completion of the Old Testament, and the beginning of the New Testament era; from about 300 B.C. to 100 B.C. Source: Stewart, D. "What Is the Old Testament Apocrypha? by Don Stewart." Blue Letter Bible. Last Modified 18 Jul 2018. https://www.blueletterbible.org/Comm/stewart_don/faq/books-missing-from-old-testament/question1-what-is-old-testament-apocrypha.cfm.

[18] Marcos, Natalio Fernández. *The Septuagint in context: Introduction to the Greek version of the Bible*, Brill, 2000, xi.

historically.[19] Its formation came more out of a necessity rather than a purposed intention.[20]

They continued steadfastly in the apostles' teaching and fellowship, in the breaking of bread, and prayer.[21]

In what we categorize as Jesus' Great Commission to His eleven disciples, He said, "...*Go and make disciples of all nations, baptizing them in the name of the Father and of the Son and of the Holy Spirit, teaching them to observe all things that I commanded you.*"[22] Jesus told them to make disciples of all nations...and to teach them to observe everything He commanded them.

Over three years, Jesus imparted specific commands for these eleven men, as well as those who would follow Him, to obey. The commands were recorded through the Gospels (Matthew, Mark, Luke, and John). And I believe the apostles' teachings were in obedience to His commission. But what we must understand is that the apostles weren't trying to create

---

[19] "Canon of the New Testament - International Standard Bible Encyclopedia," Blue Letter Bible, Last Modified 5 May, 2003, https://www.blueletterbible.org/search/Dictionary/viewTopic.cfm.

[20] Ibid.

[21] Acts 2:42.

[22] Matthew 28:19–20.

a new religion. They still considered themselves a part of the Jewish faith.[23]

When Jesus came to the earth, He did not come to overthrow the Law (Torah), He came to fulfill the messages concerning Him.[24] The Tanakh was in the apostles' hands and hearts. They were Hebrews. Israelites. Jewish men who depended on the scriptures for life and liberty in God. And it's reported that this was the case for the first century after Jesus' death.[25]

As the Gospel continued to spread through the apostles, other disciples such as Paul and Timothy began to write messages from the Lord.[26] The Old Testament continued to be used as authoritative (divinely inspired) scriptures, with increasing use from such writings after Jesus' death. The messages were slowly identified and accepted as authoritative.[27]

---

[23] Chilton, Bruce, and Jacob Neusner. *Judaism in the New Testament: Practices and beliefs*. Routledge, 2006.

[24] Luke 24:44.

[25] "Canon of the New Testament - International Standard Bible Encyclopedia," Blue Letter Bible, Last Modified 5 May, 2003, https://www.blueletterbible.org/search/Dictionary/viewTopic.cfm.

[26] "Canon of the New Testament - International Standard Bible Encyclopedia," Blue Letter Bible, Last Modified 5 May, 2003, https://www.blueletterbible.org/search/Dictionary/viewTopic.cfm.

[27] Chilton, Bruce and Jacob Neusner, *Judaism in the New Testament: Practices and Beliefs*, Routledge, New York: 1995.

What brought about what we know as the canon of the New Testament was the canon of Marcion. In the second century, Marcion was a leader of a non-orthodox[28] Christian movement.[29] In his canon, Marcion only used the writings of Paul and one Gospel, a loosely related version of Luke's book, which he edited.[30]

Marcion's canon wasn't meant to give certain books a higher authority, but rather to reject the authority of the other apostolic writings, and the Hebrew scriptures.[31] It appeared that his theology was to separate the God of Jesus from the God of Israel.[32] While some characterized Marcion as both a champion of plurality and a reformer seeking a more

---

[28] Non-orthodox is not conforming with established or accepted standards, as in religion, behaviors, or attitudes.

[29] Tyson, J. B., (2011), "Anti-Judaism in Marcion and his Opponents." *Studies in Christian-Jewish Relations*, 1(1), https://doi.org/10.6017/scjr.v1i1.1359.

[30] Ibid.

[31] Donner, Theo, "Some Thoughts On The History Of The New Testament Canon," *Themelios* 7.3 (April 1982): 23.

[32] Lieu, Judith M., *Marcion and the Making of a Heretic: God and Scripture in the Second Century,* Cambridge University Press, 2015, 71.

universal and purer type of faith, he was also seen as a heretic.[33]

Marcion's position expedited the Church's focus to establish a larger and uncorrected collection of "apostolic" writings.[34] Around 200 A.D., a New Testament existed with the four Gospels, the thirteen epistles (or letters) from Paul, 1 Peter, 1 John, and the Acts of the Apostles.[35]

Debates continued concerning the status (and inclusion) of seven books: Hebrews, James, 2 Peter, 2 and 3 John, Jude, and Revelation.[36] The Church didn't universally recognize these books. These debates continued until the fourth century when they were included in the New Testament canon.[37]

Athanasius, a bishop of Alexandria, published his thirty-ninth Festal Letter of 367. It's estimated to be the oldest document identifying all twenty-seven

[33] Foster, Paul. "Marcion: His Life, Works, Beliefs, and Impact." *The Expository Times* 121, no. 6 (March 2010): 269–80. doi:10.1177/0014524609357509, 269.

[34] Appel, Nicolaas, "The New Testament Canon: Historical Process and Spirit's Witness," *Theological Studies* 32, no. 4 (1971): 633.

[35] Ibid., 636.

[36] Donner, Theo, "Some Thoughts On The History Of The New Testament Canon," *Themelios* 7.3 (April 1982): 23.

[37] Ibid., 27.

books as the authoritative New Testament canon.[38] He used the word "canon" for these books to the exclusion of including others. Athanasius stated these books were 'fountains of salvation,' 'vital for the needs of the Church,' and concluded: "*Let no one add to them; let nothing be taken away from them.*"[39]

New Testament Canon[40]

The Gospels—Matthew, Mark, Luke, and John. The Gospels describe the birth, life, teachings, death, and resurrection of Jesus Christ.

Acts—The book of Acts follows the history of the early Church after the resurrection of Jesus Christ. It also describes the spread of Christianity throughout the known world.

The Epistles—Romans, 1 and 2 Corinthians, Galatians, Ephesians, Philippians, Colossians, 1 and 2 Thessalonians, 1 and 2 Timothy, Titus, Philemon, Hebrews, James, 1 and 2 Peter, 1, 2, and 3 John, and Jude. The epistles are letters written to many of the

---

[38] Kyrtatas, Dimitris J., "Historical Aspects of the Formation of the New Testament Canon," *Canon and Canonicity: The Formation and Use of Scripture* (2010): 29.

[39] Ibid., 47.

[40] "Books of the Bible :: Study the Divisions of the Books of the Bible." About.com Christianity. Web. 19 May, 2014. http:// christiani-ty. about.com/od/booksofthebible/tp/Books-Of-The-Bible.htm.

early churches and believers. Paul, an apostle of Jesus Christ and former persecutor of the early Church, wrote many of the epistles.[41]

Revelation. The book of Revelation is the revelation of Jesus Christ.[42] It contains prophetic messages written to describe the last days before the destruction of the earth, the punishment of the devil and his angels, and the final placement of those who are (and are not) listed in the Book of Life. It's the conclusion of God's message to His people and a message of hope for those who overcome sin and the world.

---

[41] Acts 9:1–31.

[42] Revelation 1:1.

STUDY SETTINGS

Before jumping into the Bible study methods, I wanted to share three Bible study settings for studying God's word. You might prefer one setting over another, but each can be beneficial for your personal development and growth as a disciple of Christ.

Personal Study

The personal study will probably be the first and most used study setting for studying the Bible. And as you prepare to study the Bible, please consider the following format:

Preparation. Have your Bible, study materials, and journal or application available (see Bible Study Resources). I highly encourage using a journal or note-taking app to record your answers, thoughts, and convictions. Recording your responses, ideas, and beliefs provide a foundation for individual and group study.

Prayer. Begin and end each study in prayer. Ask for God's help to prepare your heart and mind for hearing from Him and being led into all truth.[43]

Heavenly Father, I thank You for the opportunity to study Your word and learn more about being a disciple of Jesus. I humbly ask for Your help in preparing my heart and mind to study this lesson today. Please allow my heart and mind to be at peace to hear from You. In the name of Jesus Christ I pray, Amen.

Read. Take the first moments of your study to read the scripture references. You don't need to answer any lesson questions or work to complete your study quickly. Take your time. Read for understanding. Read for application.

Meditate. There's a great benefit in meditating on God's word. Think about Psalm's description of how meditating on His word is like a tree planted by streams of water. A tree near a stream of water is continually fed. It's fruitful in its season (fulfilling its purpose), and its leaf never withers (will not wear out or die). And *whatever* you do, you will prosper in it.

---

[43] Matthew 7:7–11; John 16:13; 1 John 5:14–15.

Blessed is the man who doesn't walk in the counsel of the wicked, nor stand on the path of sinners, nor sit in the seat of scoffers; but his delight is in [the LORD's] law. On his law he meditates day and night. He will be like a tree planted by the streams of water, that produces its fruit in its season, whose leaf also does not wither. Whatever he does shall prosper.[44]

Community Study

Two are better than one, because they have a good reward for their labor. For if they fall, the one will lift up his fellow; but woe to him who is alone when he falls, and doesn't have another to lift him up. Again, if two lie together, then they have warmth; but how can one keep warm alone? If a man prevails against one who is alone, two shall withstand him; and a threefold cord is not quickly broken.[45]

The beauty of the community is diversity, unity, and strength. Each person is a unique and valuable member. And through differing experiences, gifts, and perspectives, each brings a wealth of information that sharpens, encourages, and builds each person.

Within a community setting, it'll be important to interact, connect, and meet throughout the week. The

---

[44] Psalm 1:1–3.

[45] Ecclesiastes 4:9–12.

more a community can connect (via talk, text, or in-person), the higher the potential to strengthen their bonds of fellowship with one another and with Christ:

And they continued stedfastly in the apostles' doctrine and fellowship, and in breaking of bread, and in prayers. And fear came upon every soul: and many wonders and signs were done by the apostles. And all that believed were together, and had all things common; And sold their possessions and goods, and parted them to all men, as every man had need. And they, continuing daily with one accord in the temple, and breaking bread from house to house, did eat their meat with gladness and singleness of heart, Praising God, and having favour with all the people. And the Lord added to the church daily such as should be saved.[46]

The one theme in Acts 2:42–47 is *togetherness*. The believers studied together, fellowshipped together, ate together, prayed together, went to church together (daily), remained together, and had all things in common. For the early disciples, *togetherness* was an essential element for allowing the Holy Spirit to move among them and grow them personally and communally. So whether you're eating, bowling, playing cards, or sharing the highs and lows of life, being continuously connected with other like-minded disciples

---

[46] Acts 2:42–47.

can help you live and grow as a faithful Christ-follower.

Community Setting Format

As your community meets together throughout the week, there are many ways you can establish meaningful conversations and experiences. You don't need a formal structure, but the following format is but one of many examples.

Meal. When meeting together, spend time in fellowship over a meal, beverage, or dessert. Create a relaxing atmosphere with open communication. There should be no specific boundaries on your discussions, as the environment and attendees allow. Please note that not all conversations should continue where it's not beneficial or edifying in particular settings or among specific people. Please remain prayerful, sensitive to the Spirit, and aware of your surroundings. The community's purpose is for each person to receive encouragement and support as they seek to glorify the Father.

Prayer. As the meal concludes, begin your study in prayer. As you continue to meet, allow each person to have an opportunity to open and end your meetings in prayer.

What is it then, brothers? When you come together, each one of you has a psalm, has a teaching, has a rev-

elation, has another language, has an interpretation. Let all things be done to build each other up.[47]

Community Sharing. Community sharing is a time for anyone in the community to share a psalm, scripture reading, song, or any other expression of the Gospel. This is an essential time in the community. It allows community members to express their experiences with Christ outwardly.

Study. Like the personal study format, read the particular scripture references and work through any specific lesson questions or discussions. The goal here is to create an atmosphere of open dialogue. One of the ways you can do this is by asking open-ended questions in a welcoming and non-judgmental setting. Look for ways to include each community member into the discussion. Before concluding, summarize your lesson comments and discussions and reinforce ways the community can apply the lesson in their lives.

Prayer. Close your study in prayer. Before you conclude, ask if anyone has any specific prayer requests. While praying, incorporate elements of the lesson topic and discussions.

---

[47] 1 Corinthians 14:26.

Church Study

The church study encompasses elements of the personal and community studies. The church leader can use streamlined topics for both midweek, small group, and weekend messages. This approach might allow the entire church community to maintain singular themes and studies throughout each week. Church members can study individually or within smaller communities to re-enforce weekly messages and studies.

BIBLE STUDY RESOURCES

There are many resources to help you study the Bible more effectively. The number of resources in the marketplace can seem daunting, but each one has a specific purpose that can enhance your personal, community, and church Bible studies. I'll use this chapter to highlight many of these resources, most of which are free to use.[48]

Bible

There are many different Bible translations in today's marketplace.[49] I would like to suggest you find a Bible translation (or version) that helps you understand, apply, and communicate God's message. You can purchase a translation that your church endorses, pro-

---

[48] This is not an exhaustive list of resources.

[49] The translations derive from the original languages of Hebrew and Aramaic (Old Testament) and Greek (New Testament).

vides greater readability, or, most importantly, one God instructs you to use.

As Bible translations derive from the original languages of Hebrew, Aramaic, and Greek, our current English translations have several specific variations and purposes. Some translations are word-for-word or thought-for-thought translations, while others are paraphrases. Thought-for-thought and paraphrase translations are not exact translations of the original languages. They try to capture the essence or "message" the writer was trying to convey to the original audience.

Think about Bible translations like a friend translating a message in a foreign language. One friend might give you an exact translation of the message, and another friend says, "what he or she is trying to say is this..."

Bible Dictionary and Encyclopedia

Bible dictionaries and encyclopedias provide definitions and descriptions of biblical topics.

Easton's Bible Dictionary. Dr. Matthew George Easton (1823–1894) authored *Easton's Bible Dictionary*. It contains almost 4,000 entries relating to the Bible.[50]

---

[50] "Easton's Bible Dictionary," Wikipedia, Accessed June 22, 2014, http://en.m.wikipedia.org/wiki/Easton's_Bible_Dictionary.

International Standard Bible Encyclopedia. James Orr (1844–1913) was the general editor of the *International Standard Bible Encyclopedia.* The encyclopedia contains articles from almost 200 scholars. The articles cover archaeological discoveries, the language and literature of Bible lands, and Bible people's historical and religious environments.[51]

Bible Concordance

A Bible concordance is an index of biblical words, often listed in alphabetical order.

Nave's Topical Bible. Orville James Nave (1841–1917), a chaplain in the United States Army, wrote *Nave's Topical Bible. Nave's Topical Bible* is a concordance with more than 20,000 biblical topics. It also includes more than 10,000 scripture quotations indexed by subject.[52]

Strong's Concordance. Dr. James Strong (1822–1894) published *Strong's Concordance* in 1890. *Strong's Concordance* defines every Hebrew and Greek word in the King James Bible.[53] *Strong's Concordance* provides an

---

[51] "International Standard Bible Encyclopedia," Wikipedia, Accessed June 22, 2014, http://en.m.wikipedia.org/wiki/ International_Standard_Bible_Encyclopedia.

[52] "Nave's Topical Bible," Wikipedia, Accessed June 22, 2014, http:// en.m.wikipedia.org/wiki/Nave%E2%80%99s_Topical_Bible.

[53] Dr. Strong treated Hebrew and Aramaic as one language.

independent cross-check when using or comparing Bible translations. It offers the opportunity for an accurate understanding of the biblical text.[54]

Treasury of Scripture Knowledge. The *Treasury of Scripture Knowledge* provides more than 500,000 biblical cross-references.[55] The cross-references are an index of thoughts and ideas, not exact matches.[56] It also includes book summaries, chapter outlines, and alternative readings.[57]

Young's Analytical Concordance to the Bible. Robert Young (1822–1888) published *Young's Analytical Concordance to the Bible* in 1879. This concordance is suited for word studies. It analyzes English words and

[54] "Strong's Concordance," Wikipedia, Accessed June 22, 2014, https://en.wikipedia.org/wiki/Strong%27s_Concordance.

[55] "Treasury of Scripture Knowledge," Bible Study Tools, Accessed December 1, 2016, http://www.biblestudytools.com/concordances/treasury-of-scripture-knowledge/.

[56] "TSK Help Tutorial," Blue Letter Bible, Accessed December 1, 2016, https://www.blueletterbible.org/help/tsk.cfm.

[57] "The Treasury of Scripture Knowledge: Expanded with 800,000 Cross-References," SwordSearcher, Accessed December 1, 2016, http://www.swordsearcher.com/bible- study-library/treasury-of-scripture-knowledge.html.

lists scriptures containing each corresponding Hebrew or Greek word.[58]

Bible Commentary

Bible commentaries are a form of biblical exegesis. They provide explanations of biblical passages and books of the Bible.

F.B. Meyer's 'Through the Bible' Commentary. Authored by Frederick Brotherton Meyer (1847–1929), his commentary is structured as a devotional; "how to apply the Bible to your life." Commentary comments are concise, but nearly every verse in the Bible is covered, except for 1 Chronicles and parts of Numbers.[59]

Jamieson, Fausset, and Brown's Commentary. Published in 1871, Robert Jamieson (1802–1880), Andrew Robert Fausset (1821–1910), and David Brown (1803–1897) provided a detailed exegesis of the scriptures that's not overly technical but holds to the historic teachings of orthodox Christianity.[60]

---

[58] "Young's Analytical Concordance to the Bible," Wikipedia, Accessed December 8, 2016, https://en.wikipedia.org/wiki/Young's_Analytical_Concordance_to_the_Bible.

[59] "Overview - F.B. Meyer's 'Through the Bible' Commentary," Studylight, Accessed February 11, 2020, https://www.studylight.org/commentaries/jfb.html.

[60] "Overview - Jamieson, Fausset and Brown's Commentary Critical and Explanatory on the Whole Bible," Studylight, Accessed February 11, 2020, https://www.studylight.org/commentaries/jfb.html.

Matthew Henry's Complete Bible Commentary. This concordance provides an exhaustive verse-by-verse study of the Bible.[61]

Bible Software and Websites

Bible software and websites provide libraries of biblical resources. They offer several ways to understand, apply, and communicate God's word.

YouVersion. YouVersion is the ministry of Life.Church. YouVersion's purpose is to provide a free Bible for every phone, tablet, and computer.[62] Through its website, Bible.com, and application, YouVersion provides over 1,400 Bible translations supporting 1,071 languages.[63]

e-Sword. e-Sword is a Bible study application and computer program created by Rick Meyers in 2000. e-Sword provides Bible translations, a reference library, audio sermons, and much more.[64]

---

[61] "Matthew Henry," Wikipedia, Accessed June 22, 2014, http:// en.wikipedia.org/wiki/Matthew_Henry.

[62] "Resources & Applications for Churches | Life.Church," Life.Church, Accessed January 25, 2017, http:// www.life.church/ churches/?utm_ source=life.church.

[63] "YouVersion" YouVersion, Accessed January 25, 2017, https:// www.youversion.com.

[64] "Features," e-Sword, Accessed November 29, 2016, http://www.e-sword.net/index.html#features.

Bible Gateway. Nick Hengeveld created Bible Gateway in 1993. Bible Gateway provides a website and application with over 50 Bible translations, advanced search tools, and other biblical resources.[65]

Bible Hub. Bible Hub began as an online platform in 2004 through the Online Parallel Bible Project. Bible Hub has a three-purpose mission:

1. increase the visibility and accessibility of the scriptures online,

2. provide free access to Bible study tools in many languages,

3. promote the Gospel through the learning, study, and application of God's word.[66]

Blue Letter Bible. The Blue Letter Bible Project is an initiative of Sowing Circle Ministries. Blue Letter Bible provides three ongoing efforts:

1. CDs for missionaries, pastors, and students,

2. a website for online Bible studies,

---

[65] "BibleGateway.com," Wikipedia, Accessed November 29, 2016, https://en.wikipedia.org/wiki/BibleGateway.com.

[66] "About Us," Bible Hub, Accessed November 29, 2016, http://biblehub.com/about.htm.

3. an institute for structured biblical studies.[67]

OpenBible.info. OpenBible.info provides several biblical resources, such as a topical Bible, Bible maps, and cross-references of the Bible. OpenBible.info also has a *lab* for conducting small experiments using biblical data.

---

[67] "Blue Letter Bible," Wikipedia, Accessed November 29, 2016, https://en.wikipedia.org/wiki/Blue_Letter_Bible.

PASSAGE STUDY

The passage study is one of the most common Bible studies many Christians will conduct. A passage study reviews biblical passages to understand its historical and personal context. The historical and personal context goes back to exegesis. You want to first understand the author's original message to its audience before applying any personal applications.

Historical Context

The historical context can help you identify a source scripture's intended message to its original audience.[68] As the Bible describes events occurring thousands of years ago, understanding the historical context will keep you from misinterpreting scriptures. This helps you to conduct a proper exegesis.

---

[68] A source scripture is the subject of a particular Bible study.

This is what being a workman approved by God who doesn't need to be ashamed means.[69] And to help you conduct a good passage study, I'd like for you to think in terms of street, city, and state views. These will represent our expanding study of scriptures.

Street View

The street view represents a review of scriptures before and after a source scripture in the same chapter. These verses are most connected to your source scripture and might provide immediate context to the message delivered.

To see how this works, let's use Matthew 6:8 as an example source scripture:

Therefore don't be like them, for your Father knows what things you need, before you ask him.

For the street view, I would review the verses before and after this source scripture but in the same chapter, Matthew 6. Beginning at Matthew 6:1, I found that verses 1–4 address giving and verses 5–7 address prayer:

Verses 1–4:

Be careful that you don't do your charitable giving before men, to be seen by them, or else you have no

---

[69] 2 Timothy 2:15.

reward from your Father who is in heaven. Therefore when you do merciful deeds, don't sound a trumpet before yourself, as the hypocrites do in the synagogues and in the streets, that they may get glory from men. Most certainly I tell you, they have received their reward. But when you do merciful deeds, don't let your left hand know what your right hand does, so that your merciful deeds may be in secret, then your Father who sees in secret will reward you openly.

Verses 5–7:

When you pray, you shall not be as the hypocrites, for they love to stand and pray in the synagogues and in the corners of the streets, that they may be seen by men. Most certainly, I tell you, they have received their reward. But you, when you pray, enter into your inner room, and having shut your door, pray to your Father who is in secret, and your Father who sees in secret will reward you openly. In praying, don't use vain repetitions, as the Gentiles do; for they think that they will be heard for their much speaking.

When reviewing the verses after Matthew 6:8, I discovered a continued discussion on prayer through verse 13:

Pray like this: 'Our Father in heaven, may your name be kept holy. Let your Kingdom come. Let your will be done, as in heaven, so on earth. Give us today our daily bread. Forgive us our debts, as we also forgive our debtors. Bring us not into temptation, but deliver us from the evil one. For yours is the Kingdom, the power, and the glory forever. Amen.'

Because Matthew 6:5–13 spoke about prayer, my street view of the source scripture helped me understand the context of Matthew 6:8. If I read beyond verse 13, the discussion changes to forgiveness and other topics. But if I want to learn more about the source scripture within an expanded context of what Jesus was saying, I'll need to enlarge my view.

City View

The second view is the city view. This view looks at Bible chapters surrounding a source scripture within a book of the Bible. A city view can provide a greater understanding, context, and perspective of the source scripture, as well as broader topics and discussions within a book of the Bible.

To begin a city view, I'll read one chapter before and one chapter after the source scripture. I'll expand to other chapters as necessary to either capture a greater understanding of the source scripture or learn more about different subjects mentioned in that specific book.

With our source scripture in Matthew 6:8, I started my city view at Matthew 5:1. I found that the source scripture is a part of Jesus' teaching to His disciples and the multitudes.[70] Now, I can read Matthew 4 to find out what Jesus was doing before this, but I want to learn more about Jesus' teaching mentioned in Matthew 5:1 and where it concluded. After reading Matthew 6–7, I discovered that His teaching ended at Matthew 7:28.

How did I learn this?

Help and Resources

As I conduct street, city, and state views of scriptures, biblical resources can enhance my studies. I'll use several biblical references to increase my understanding of Matthew 6:8 and the surrounding scriptures.

Treasury of Scripture Knowledge

The *Treasury of Scripture Knowledge* uses a chapter-by-chapter review of the Bible. This focus can help me for both street and city views.

To see how this works, I'll start at Matthew 6:1. The corresponding entry states, "*Christ continues his sermon on the mount, exhorting not to be careful for*

---

[70] Matthew 5:1.

worldly things."[71] If I conduct a wider city view of Matthew 6:8 to Matthew 5 and Matthew 7, the *Treasury of Scripture Knowledge's* entry for Matthew 5:1 reads, "*Christ's sermon on the mount.*"[72] The entry for Matthew 7:28 reads, "*Christ ends his sermon, and the people are astonished.*"[73] These entries frame the context of the source scripture of Matthew 6:8.

Bible Dictionaries and Encyclopedias

Bible dictionaries and encyclopedias such as *Easton's Bible Dictionary* and the *International Standard Bible Encyclopedia* allow me to learn about the book of Matthew, as well as specific people, places, and concepts in the Bible.

When using *Easton's Bible Dictionary* for this study, I learned how the book of Matthew was written to prove that Jesus of Nazareth was the promised Messiah and that in Him, the ancient prophecies had their fulfillment. I also learned about the probable

---

[71] "Matthew 6:1," Bible Study Tools, Accessed January 4, 2018, https://www.biblestudytools.com/concordances/ treasury-of-scripture-knowledge/matthew-6-1.html.

[72] "Matthew 5:1," Bible Study Tools, Accessed December 6, 2016, http://www.biblestudytools.com/concordances/treasury- of-scripture-knowledge/matthew-5-1.html.

[73] "Matthew 7:28," Bible Study Tools, Accessed January 29, 2016, http://www.biblestudytools.com/concordances/treasury- of-scripture-knowledge/matthew-7-29.html.

times the book was written as well as discovering the possible location of Jesus' sermon.[74]

After reviewing the *International Standard Bible Encyclopedia*, I found the following section about the source scripture:[75]

(a) In Worship (Matthew 6:1–18):

In the section Mt 6:1 through 7:12 there is one central thought. All righteousness looks toward God. He is at once the source and the aim of life. Therefore worship aims alone at divine praise. If acts of worship are performed before men to be seen of them there is no reward for them before the Father. In this Jesus is passing no slight on public worship. He Himself instituted the Lord's Supper and authorized the continuance of the rite of baptism. Such acts have their proper value. His censure is aimed at the love of ostentation so often associated with them. The root of ostentation is selfishness, and selfishness has no part in the new righteousness. Any selfish desire for the approval of men thwarts the purpose of all worship. The object of almsgiving, of prayer or of fasting is the expression of brotherly love, communion with God or

---

[74] "New Testament Holy Land—Matthew," Blue Letter Bible, Accessed December 6, 2016, https://www.blueletterbible.org/assets/images/BibleMedia/rosepub/maps_nt.png.

[75] "Sermon on the Mount," Bible Hub, Accessed February 13, 2020, https://bibleapps.com/s/sermon_on_the_mount.htm.

spiritual enrichment. The possibility of any of these is excluded by the presence of the desire for the approval of men. It is not merely a divine fiat but one of the deeper laws of life which decrees that the only possible reward for acts of worship performed from such false motives is the cheap approval of men as well as the impoverishment of the inner life.

Cross-References and Concordances

Cross-references and concordances provide additional views of corresponding words and scriptures relating to the source scripture or topic. This can be a great benefit for finding similar messages that connect throughout the Bible. But there are times when specific cross-references aren't a direct match to your source scripture or what you're looking for, and that's okay. Remember, your reviews are a part of a larger discovery of learning more about God and His message to you and others.

So returning to the *Treasury of Scripture Knowledge*, there are several corresponding scriptures listed under *your* in Matthew 6:8:[76]

Psalm 38:9—*Lord, all my desire is before you. My groaning is not hidden from you.*

---

[76] "Treasury of Scripture Knowledge," Bible Study Tools, Accessed December 1, 2016, http://www.biblestudytools.com/concordances/treasury-of-scripture-knowledge.

Psalm 69:17–19—*Don't hide your face from your servant, for I am in distress. Answer me speedily! Draw near to my soul, and redeem it. Ransom me because of my enemies. You know my reproach, my shame, and my dishonor. My adversaries are all before you.*

Matthew 6:32—*For the Gentiles seek after all these things; for your heavenly Father knows that you need all these things.*

Luke 12:30—*For the nations of the world seek after all of these things, but your Father knows that you need these things.*

John 16:23–27—*In that day you will ask me no questions. Most certainly I tell you, whatever you may ask of the Father in my name, he will give it to you. Until now, you have asked nothing in my name. Ask, and you will receive, that your joy may be made full. I have spoken these things to you in figures of speech. But the time is coming when I will no more speak to you in figures of speech, but will tell you plainly about the Father. In that day you will ask in my name; and I don't say to you, that I will pray to the Father for you, for the Father himself loves you, because you have loved me, and have believed that I came from God.*

Philippians 4:6—*In nothing be anxious, but in everything, by prayer and petition with thanksgiving, let your requests be made known to God.*

Reviewing cross-references from OpenBible.info, I also found the following references:[77]

Psalm 17:14—*from men by your hand, [LORD], from men of the world, whose portion is in this life. You fill the belly of your cherished ones. Your sons have plenty, and they store up wealth for their children.*

Psalm 103:13—*Like a father has compassion on his children, so [the LORD] has compassion on those who fear him.*

Matthew 5:46–47—*For if you love those who love you, what reward do you have? Don't even the tax collectors do the same? If you only greet your friends, what more do you do than others? Don't even the tax collectors do the same?*

Matthew 20:25–26—*But Jesus summoned them, and said, "You know that the rulers of the nations lord it over them, and their great ones exercise authority over them. It shall not be so among you, but whoever desires to become great among you shall be your servant.*

---

[77] "Matthew 6:8 Cross References," Openbible.info, Accessed December 6, 2016, https://www.openbible.info/labs/cross-references/search?q=Matthew+6%3A8.

Luke 11:11–13— *"Which of you fathers, if your son asks for bread, will give him a stone? Or if he asks for a fish, he won't give him a snake instead of a fish, will he? Or if he asks for an egg, he won't give him a scorpion, will he? If you then, being evil, know how to give good gifts to your children, how much more will your heavenly Father give the Holy Spirit to those who ask him?"*

Ephesians 4:17— *This I say therefore, and testify in the Lord, that you no longer walk as the rest of the Gentiles also walk, in the futility of their mind,*

1 Thessalonians 4:5— *not in the passion of lust, even as the Gentiles who don't know God;*

Concordances

When I'm looking to find a Hebrew (Old Testament) or Greek (New Testament) definition in an English Bible, one of the first references I reach for is *Strong's Concordance.*

One of several ways I can access *Strong's Concordance* is through the Bible Hub website. To begin, I go to the Bible Hub website and type, "Matthew 6:8" in the main search bar. I click on the Greek button at the top of the page to view *Strong's Concordance.* If I use e-Sword, I would download the King James Bible with *Strong's Concordance* (KJV+). Then, after going to Matthew 6:8, I would select the KJV+ Bible to review *need* and *knoweth*:

Need—From the base of G5530 or G5534; employment, that is, an affair; also (by implication) occasion, demand, requirement or destitution: - business, lack, necessary (-ity), need (-ful), use, want.

Knowest—A primary verb; used only in certain past tenses, the others being borrowed from the equivalent, G3700 and G3708; properly to see (literally or figuratively); by implication (in the perfect only) to know: - be aware, behold, X can (+ not tell), consider, (have) known (-ledge), look (on), perceive, see, be sure, tell, understand, wist, wot. Compare G3700.

Commentaries

To receive additional comments, thoughts, and perspectives about Matthew 6:8, I can select *Text Commentaries* under the Study heading on Bible Hub. There are several commentaries to choose from, so I select *Jamieson, Fausett & Brown*. Within their commentary for Matthew 6, the entry for Matthew 6:8 states:[78]

---

[78] Source: "Commentary on Matthew 6 by Jamieson, Fausett & Brown," Blue Letter Bible, Accessed December 17, 2017, https://www.blueletterbible.org/Comm/jfb/Mat/Mat_006.cfm.

8. Be not ye therefore like unto them: for your Father knoweth what things ye have need of before ye ask him —and so needs not to be informed of our wants, any more than to be roused to attend to them by our incessant speaking. What a view of God is here given, in sharp contrast with the gods of the heathen! But let it be carefully noted that it is not as the general Father of mankind that our Lord says, "Your Father" knoweth what ye need before ye ask it; for it is not men, as such, that He is addressing in this discourse, but His own disciples—the poor in spirit, the mourners, the meek, hungry and thirsty souls, the merciful, the pure in heart, the peacemakers, who allow themselves to have all manner of evil said against them for the Son of man's sake—in short, the new-born children of God, who, making their Father's interests their own, are here assured that their Father, in return, makes their interests His, and needs neither to be told nor to be reminded of their wants. Yet He will have His children pray to Him, and links all His promised supplies to their petitions for them; thus encouraging us to draw near and keep near to Him, to talk and walk with Him, to open our every case to Him, and assure ourselves that thus asking we shall receive—thus seeking we shall find—thus knocking it shall be opened to us.*

State View

The state view reviews biblical books surrounding a source scripture. This view can help you see how the books of the Bible *connect* to tell a specific story to its readers.

For this exercise, I would like to learn if there are any parallel stories of Matthew 6:8 in the Gospels. After reviewing additional information about the Sermon on the Mount in *Easton's Bible Dictionary* and the *International Standard Bible Encyclopedia*, I found that Luke 6:20–49 is a possible parallel to Matthew 5–7. But in further review, Luke 6:20–49 is not a parallel message to Matthew 6:8.[79]

Historical Context

Lord willing, you were able to see how the street, city, and state views can help you gain a greater understanding of a source scripture's historical context. And with the information you collect, you can evaluate the source scripture and conduct a proper exegesis. So now I'll show you how I've

---

[79] The Bible is not a complete historical record of every event since the creation of the world. God inspired each author to provide a specific aspect or perspective of His story (2 Timothy 3:16; 2 Peter 1:20–21). Please don't assume or add specific information where it might not be clearly identified.

constructed my exegesis using the *Who*, *What*, *Where*, *Why*, *When*, and *How* format:

Who—Jesus was talking to His disciples and the multitudes who followed Him from Galilee, the Decapolis, Jerusalem, Judea, and beyond the Jordan.[80]

What—Jesus was speaking about prayer. He said you should not be like the heathens, who use vain repetitions.[81] They believe they'll be heard because of their many words. However, your Father already knows what you need before you ask Him.

Where—The one fact we have is that Jesus went up into a mountain. Jesus was in Galilee before and after His sermon. His teaching most likely occurred in Galilee, but the scriptures don't specify the location.

Why—Jesus' sermon was a continuation of His preaching and teaching throughout Galilee from Matthew 4:23–25.

When—According to the Bible Hub website, the approximate date for the Sermon on the Mount was 27 A.D.[82]

---

[80] Matthew 4:23–25.

[81] Matthew 6:7.

[82] "Bible Timeline," Bible Hub, Accessed December 6, 2016, http://biblehub.com/timeline/new.htm.

How—Jesus went up into the mountain and sat down to teach His disciples and the multitude.[83]

Personal Context

The last step in the passage study is learning if there are any personal applications for your life. Throughout the Bible, you'll find that not every verse is meant for personal application. Some scriptures and promises are only intended for a specific group of people or represent historical information. And a proper exegesis will help you determine that.

So from the historical context of Matthew 6:8, I learned two things that can be applied in my life. First, I should not pray like the heathens, who use vain repetitions. Now, I can pray about a matter continually because Jesus directs us to,[84] but the keywords here are *vain repetitions*, which are meaningless. Second, my Father knows what I need even before I ask Him.

---

[83] Matthew 5:1–2.

[84] Luke 18:1–8.

WORD STUDY

My first in-depth experience with word studies came in 1999. I spent five years building a library of over five hundred biblical topics. This library has been a foundational staple in my life as a disciple of Jesus. The benefit of having a personal, at-your-fingertips resource has been invaluable. Even after two decades, I return to it again and again...and again. So, let's check out a couple of ways you can conduct word and topic searches.

Word Search

To begin our word study, let's start with Job 42:6:

Wherefore I abhor myself, and repent in dust and ashes.

To conduct a word search on *abhor,* I can look up *abhor* in a standard dictionary, but I want to get as close as possible to the description Job used. So I'll use two concordances for my search: *Strong's Concordance* and *Young's Analytical Concordance to the Holy Bible.*

Strong's Concordance. When searching Job 42:6 in *Strong's Concordance*, the Hebrew root word for *abhor* is *'em-'as,* which means *despise.*

Young's Analytical Concordance to the Holy Bible. *Abhor* has eleven Hebrew references from the Old Testament. The entry for Job 42:6 describes *abhor* as *despise, reject, or loathe.*

That's it. There's not much in completing a word search. The only difference is in the biblical resource you use to find your definitions.

Topic Search

Topic searches help you learn about scriptures covering a specific topic within a biblical book or across the Bible. The two topic searches you can conduct are internal or external.

Internal Topic Search

An internal topic search occurs without the help of a pre-populated biblical reference, such as a concordance or dictionary. For example, I'll conduct an internal topic search on the subject of *grace* in the New Testament. On the Bible Gateway website, a keyword search of *grace* produces 122 references from the King James Bible.[85] After conducting street and city views for each reference, I discovered five provisions of grace listed in the Bible:

1. Unmerited favor (Romans 5:12–15; Titus 3:4–7).

2. Redemption (Romans 3:24–25; Ephesians 2:8).

3. Teaching and instruction (Titus 2:11–14).

4. A place of mercy and help (Hebrews 4:15–16).

5. Power and sufficiency (2 Corinthians 9:8, 12:9–10).

External Topic Search

External topic searches use pre-populated biblical references, such as a Bible concordance or dictionary. Using *Nave's Topical Bible* for the external topic search on *grace*, I found one entry on the *Grace of God* as follows:[86]

General references

Gen 15:6; Gen 20:6; Deu 7:6–9; Deu 9:4–6; Job 10:12; Job 22:2–3; Psa 94:17–19; Psa 138:3; Psa 143:11; Dan 9:18;

---

[85] "Bible Gateway: grace," Bible Gateway, Accessed December 6, 2016, https://www.biblegateway.com/quicksearch/?quicksearch=grace &q s_version=KJV.

[86] e-Sword Bible Program, Accessed December 12, 2016, http://www.e-sword.net.

Dan 10:18–19; Joh 6:44–45; Joh 17:11–12; Joh 17:15; Act 4:29–30; Act 26:22; Rom 3:22–24; Rom 4:4; Rom 4:16; Rom 5:2; Rom 5:6–8; Rom 5:15–21; Rom 9:10–16; Rom 11:5–6; 1Co 1:4–8; 1Co 10:13; 1Co 15:10; 2Co 1:12; Gal 1:15–16; Eph 1:5–9; Eph 1:11–12; Eph 2:8–9; Eph 3:16; Eph 4:7; Eph 6:10; Php 1:19; Php 2:13; 1Th 1:1; 1Th 5:28; 2Pe 1:2; 1Ti 1:14; 2Ti 1:1; 2Ti 1:9; Tit 3:7; 1Pe 1:5; 1Pe 4:10; 1Pe 5:10; Jud 1:1; Jud 1:21; Jud 1:24–25; Rev 3:10

Growth in

Psa 84:7; Pro 4:18; Php 1:6; Php 1:9–11; Php 3:12–15; Col 1:10–11; Col 2:19; 1Th 3:10; 1Th 3:12–13; 2Th 1:3; Heb 6:1–3; 1Pe 2:1–3; 2Pe 3:18

OUTLINE STUDY

Outlines provide summary overviews of scripture passages and books of the Bible. They identify scriptural information in a condensed format. There are many biblical outlines available, such as *The Outline Bible* by Harold L. Wilmington, *Matthew Henry's Complete Bible Commentary*, and the *Treasury of Scripture Knowledge*.

As a minister, I love using outlines for my website and the messages I preach and teach. Outlines organize my messages in a structured format and flow.

To begin our outline study, let's use Psalm 1 as an example:

1 *Blessed is the man who doesn't walk in the counsel of the wicked, nor stand on the path of sinners, nor sit in the seat of scoffers;*

2 *but his delight is in [the LORD's] law. On his law he meditates day and night.*

3 *He will be like a tree planted by the streams of water, that produces its fruit in its season, whose leaf also does not wither. Whatever he does shall prosper.*

4 *The wicked are not so, but are like the chaff which the wind drives away.*

5 *Therefore the wicked shall not stand in the judgment, nor sinners in the congregation of the righteous.*

6 *For [the LORD] knows the way of the righteous, but the way of the wicked shall perish.*

Here are outlines of Psalm 1 from the *Treasury of Scripture Knowledge* and *The Outline Bible*:

Treasury of Scripture Knowledge:[87]

Overview—Psalms 1

1 The happiness of the godly.

4 The unhappiness of the ungodly.

---

[87] "Treasury of Scripture Knowledge," Bible Study Tools, Accessed December 1, 2016, http://www.biblestudytools.com/ concordances/ treasury-of-scripture- knowledge.

The Outline Bible:[88]

Section Outline One (Psalm 1)

The psalmist compares and contrasts the godly and the wicked and notes the eventual end of each.

I. The godly (1:1–3)

A. The contrast (1:1–2)

1. What they do not do (1:1)

a. Follow the advice of the wicked.

b. Stand around with sinners.

c. Join in with scoffers.

2. What they do (1:2): they delight in the law of the Lord.

B. The comparison (1:3): they are like fruitful, well-watered trees.

II. The godless (1:4–6): The Lord protects the godly, but the wicked are worthless chaff which will one day be condemned and destroyed.

---

[88] Harold L. Wilmington, *The Outline Bible* (Wheaton, IL: Tyndale House, 1999), 221.

Did you notice the difference in the details with these references? Having too much or too little information in an outline is neither right nor wrong. Use a biblical reference that provides the information and details you're looking for.

Now, let's review three outlines you can prepare for your studies: simple, detailed, and point. As you go through this section and practice on your own, remember *proper exegesis*. Remain committed to developing an accurate interpretation of the scriptures you're outlining.

Simple Outline

A simple outline provides main ideas from a source scripture in a concise format. There are two points to consider when building a simple outline:

1. Meditate. When creating an outline, it's important to first meditate on the source scripture. The Bible defines *meditate* in Psalm 1:2 from the original Hebrew language as:

ponder—think about (something) carefully, especially before making a decision or reaching a conclusion,

imagine—form a mental image or concept of,

speak—say something to convey information, an opinion, or a feeling, *study*—the devotion of time and attention to acquiring knowledge on an academic subject, especially using books; a detailed investigation and analysis of a subject or situation,

talk—speak to give information or express ideas or feelings; converse or communicate by spoken words.

As you might notice, meditation requires an investment of time, thoughts, and even communication to understand a biblical passage. Meditation is an all-day engagement of the scriptures that leads you to success and brings fruit in its season.[89]

2. Identify the main ideas. Determine what stories, subjects, or messages the source scripture is describing. Search for specific words that point out the main ideas.

After reading Psalm 1, I identified four subjects: blessed, wicked, sinner, and righteous. Then, I structured my outline in the following manner:

(1:1–3)—The life of a blessed man.

(1:4)—The life of the wicked.

(1:5)—Where the wicked and sinners cannot stand.

---

[89] Joshua 1:8; Psalm 1:2–3.

(1:6)—The way of the righteous and wicked.

You might notice my outline is different from *The Treasury of Scripture Knowledge* and *The Outline Bible.* But my outline is still faithful to the content in Psalm 1. Again, no one way is right or wrong as long as you provide an accurate summary of the source scripture.

Detailed Outline

A detailed outline adds supporting information to a simple outline. To develop my detailed outline for Psalm 1, I'll take my four subject areas and ask these questions to gather the necessary information for my outline: *who, what, where, why, when,* and *how.* As an example, how does Psalm 1:1–2 describe the life of a blessed man?

Blessed is the man who doesn't walk in the counsel of the wicked, nor stand on the path of sinners, nor sit in the seat of scoffers; but his delight is in [the LORD's] law. On his law he meditates day and night.[90]

(1:1–2)—The life of a blessed man:

A blessed man doesn't walk in the counsel of the wicked.

---

[90] Psalm 1:1–2.

A blessed man doesn't stand on the path of sinners.

A blessed man doesn't sit in the seat of scoffers.

A blessed man's delight is in the Lord's law.

A blessed man meditates on the Lord's law day and night.

When developing a detailed outline, add as many accurate details as you desire or need. Now, I don't think you should provide so much detail that you rewrite the scripture reference, but it shouldn't resemble a simple outline. Strike a balance that stays true to the text with useful supporting information. Here's my complete detailed outline for Psalm 1:

(1:1–3)—The life of a blessed man:

A blessed man doesn't walk in the counsel of the wicked.

A blessed man doesn't stand on the path of sinners.

A blessed man doesn't sit in the seat of scoffers.

A blessed man's delight is in the Lord's law.

A blessed man meditates on the Lord's law day and night.

Through this (see 1:1–2):

> He will be like a tree planted by the rivers of water that brings forth its fruit in its season.

> His leaf will not wither.

> Whatever he does will prosper.

(1:4)—The life of the wicked:

> The wicked are not like the blessed.

> The wicked are like the chaff that the wind drives away.

(1:5)—Where the wicked and sinners cannot stand:

> Because of this (see 1:4):

>> The wicked shall not stand in the judgment.

>> Sinners shall not stand in the congregation of the righteous.

(1:6)—The way of the righteous and wicked:

> The reason for 1:5:

>> The Lord knows the way of the righteous.

>> The way of the wicked shall perish.

Point Outline

Point outlines identify a specific subject or theme found in a source scripture. So using the detailed outline, I'll begin with Psalm 1:1–2, *The life of a blessed man*, to build a new point outline heading:

1. A blessed man doesn't walk in the counsel of the wicked.

2. A blessed man doesn't stand on the path of sinners.

3. A blessed man doesn't sit in the seat of scoffers.

4. A blessed man's delight is in the Lord's law.

5. A blessed man meditates on the Lord's law day and night.

Looking at this information, you might see a common theme in this outline: a blessed man. And as the listing describes five different characteristics or attributes, I believe I've found an appropriate heading:

Five Attributes of a Blessed Man

And if you look further, there might be other subjects or themes you can describe, such as three places not to be or two things a blessed man will do with the Lord's law. So as I stated, there are many ways to develop your point outline. It's only limited by your meditation and development of the text. Here's my complete point outline for Psalm 1:

Five Attributes of a Blessed Man

1. He doesn't walk in the counsel of the wicked.

2. He doesn't stand in the way of sinners.

3. He doesn't sit in the seat of scoffers.

4. His delight is in the Lord's law.

5. He meditates on the Lord's law day and night.

Three Benefits of a Blessed Man

1. He shall be like a tree planted by the streams of water that produces its fruit in its season.

2. The tree's leaves will not wither.

3. Whatever he does will prosper.

Two Outcomes of the Wicked and One for the Sinner

1. The wicked are like the chaff, which the wind drives away.

2. The wicked shall not stand in the judgment.

3. Sinners shall not stand in the congregation of the righteous.

Two Ways the Lord Knows

1. The Lord knows the way of the righteous.

2. The way of the wicked shall perish.

PERSONAL PROFILE STUDY

Personal profile studies are like biographies. These studies highlight the lives of specific individuals from the Bible. They often provide historical information or identify life lessons or principles in a summary format. The following pages identify three criteria to consider when building a personal profile study.

Purpose

Your purpose will guide every aspect of your study. Your audience will drive your purpose and the information you present. Since my goal in this chapter is to explain what a personal profile study is, I'd like to use a personal profile on the man of God from 1 Kings 13.

Information Collection

With your purpose solidified, it's time to collect the information to help you construct your profile. Using the information you've read in this book, you've gained the necessary tools to accomplish your purpose.

For my study on the man of God from 1 Kings 13, I plan to conduct a city view of 1 Kings 11-13 because he's first introduced in 1 Kings 11. 1 Kings 11-12 provides the background information surrounding his story.

Presentation

After determining your purpose and collecting your information, prepare your information. If you gather a large quantity of information, don't feel obligated to add every detail. Some details might detract from your purpose but remember *proper exegesis*. So without further delay, here's my profile study on the man of God from 1 Kings 13:

After obtaining 700 wives and 300 concubines, King Solomon's wives turned his heart after other gods. He did evil in the sight of the Lord, and his heart turned away from the Lord twice. As a result, the Lord told

Solomon He would tear all but one of the twelve tribes of Israel from his son when he became king.[91]

The Lord also sent adversaries against Solomon. Jeroboam, an adversary, in particular, received a prophecy that he would become king of ten of the twelve tribes of Israel that would be torn from Solomon's son. Though Solomon sought to kill him, Jeroboam fled to Egypt until Solomon died.

After Solomon's death, Israel appointed his son, Rehoboam, as king. Jeroboam returned to Israel, and he and all the people of Israel came before the king. They asked if he would lighten the yoke his father had laid on the people. Rehoboam asked for three days to respond. Instead of listening to the older men who stood before his father, he accepted the counsel of those he grew up with.

On the third day, Jeroboam and all the people came to Rehoboam. Rehoboam said he would add to their yoke. He would discipline them with scorpions rather than the whips his father used. When the people heard this, they returned to their tents and made Jeroboam king over the ten tribes of Israel.

---

[91] This excluded the tribe of Levi, who were priests and ministers before the tabernacle unto God and Israel (Numbers 1:50–53, 3:6–51, 18:1–32; Deuteronomy 10:9, 18:1–8).

As a ruler over Israel, Jeroboam was concerned about the people. He thought they might return to Rehoboam if they went up to offer sacrifices in Jerusalem.[92] He took counsel and made two golden calves (as gods) to which the people could offer sacrifices. This led the people into sin. Jeroboam also built temples on the high places[93] and appointed priests who were not sons of Levi.[94]

Jeroboam also devised a feast from his own heart.[95] He appointed a feast for the people of Israel (like the feast in Judah) on the fifteenth day of the eighth month. On this day, he went up to Bethel and

---

[92] Jerusalem was a city within the tribe of Judah where Rehoboam was still king.

[93] *Easton's Bible Dictionary* describes a high place as an eminence, natural or artificial, where worship by sacrifice or offerings was made (1 Kings 13:32; 2 Kings 17:29). After the Israelites entered the Promised Land they were strictly enjoined to overthrow the high places of the Canaanites (Exodus 34:13; Deuteronomy 7:5; 12:2, 3), and they were forbidden to worship the Lord on high places (Deuteronomy 12:11–14), and were enjoined to use but one altar for sacrifices (Leviticus 17:3,4; Deuteronomy 12; 16:21). The injunction against high places was, however, very imperfectly obeyed, and we find again and again, mention made of them (2 Kings 14:4; 2 Chronicles 15:17).

[94] Priests were only to be selected from the tribe of Levi (Deuteronomy 10:8; 18:5).

[95] *Matthew Henry's Complete Bible Commentary* states the feast of tabernacles, which God had appointed on the fifteenth day of the seventh month, [Jeroboam] adjourned to the fifteenth day of the eighth month (1 Kings 12:32), the month which he devised of his own heart, to show his power in ecclesiastical matters, 1 Kings 12:33.

sacrificed to the calves he made and went to the altar to burn incense.[96]

As Jeroboam stood by the altar to burn incense, a man of God came from Judah. He came by the word of the Lord to cry out against the altar Jeroboam had made. The man of God said, "*Altar! Altar! [The LORD] says: 'Behold, a son will be born to David's house, Josiah by name. On you he will sacrifice the priests of the high places who burn incense on you, and they will burn men's bones on you.*" The man of God also provided a sign, saying, "*This is the sign which [the LORD] has spoken: Behold, the altar will be split apart, and the ashes that are on it will be poured out.*"

When Jeroboam heard the man of God, he stretched out his hand from the altar, saying, "*Lay hold on him.*" However, Jeroboam's hand dried up, and he couldn't draw it back to himself. Then the altar was split apart, and the ashes poured out as the man of God described.

Jeroboam asked the man of God to intercede for the Lord's favor and pray for the Lord to restore his hand. The man of God interceded, and the Lord restored Jeroboam's hand. Jeroboam asked the man of God to come home with him to refresh himself and receive a

---

[96] Jeroboam broke the first and second commandments given to Israel in Exodus 20:3–6.

reward. The man of God said that even if he received half of Jeroboam's house, he wouldn't go into his home. The man of God also stated he would not eat nor drink water in Bethel. The Lord commanded him not to eat bread or drink water nor return by the way he came. So the man of God departed and followed the Lord's instructions.

Now, there was an old prophet who lived in Bethel. His sons told him everything the man of God had done in the city and the words he spoke to Jeroboam. After learning the direction the man of God traveled, the old prophet went after him. Finding the man of God under an oak tree, he invited him to his house to eat bread. The man of God repeated the same words he said to Jeroboam. The old prophet told the man of God that he was also a prophet. But he lied and said an angel spoke to him. He said the angel told him the man of God should return to his house and eat bread and drink water with him. Upon hearing this, the man of God went back with him, ate bread, and drank water.

As they sat at the table, the word of the Lord came to the old prophet. He cried to the man of God saying, "*The LORD says, 'Because you have been disobedient to [the LORD's] mouth, and have not kept the commandment which [the LORD] your God commanded you, but came back, and have eaten bread*

*and drank water in the place of which he said to you,
"Eat no bread, and drink no water;" your body will
not come to the tomb of your fathers."'*

After departing the old prophet's house, a lion killed
the man of God. When the old prophet found out
what happened, he said it was the man of God who
disobeyed the word of the Lord. He went out and
found the man of God's body thrown in the road
with his donkey and the lion standing next to his
body. The lion didn't eat the man of God's body nor
tear the donkey. The old prophet placed the man of
God's body on his donkey and returned to the city to
mourn and bury him. He buried the man of God in
his own grave by the word of the Lord spoken
through the old prophet.

Life Lesson

With many personal profiles, there might be a specific
life lesson you want to share with your intended
audience. This is based on your purpose. Though you
might share a proper exegesis of the biblical text, what
you provide in your summary from your profile
might be a principle or lesson from the text.

From my personal profile study on the man of God, I
wanted to highlight a "*lesson*" we can learn from the
biblical text:

Remain committed to the message God speaks to you. If someone speaks conflicting information, first receive a personal confirmation from the Lord. You must be sure of any change or deviation because you will account for your own actions of obedience or disobedience.

While studying a personal profile, you'll learn a wealth of information about other biblical personalities and subjects. As I studied about the man of God, I learned how the decisions of five men impacted either themselves or those they held influence or authority over. And as a result, I believe it's important we consider the choices we make and their potential consequences to ourselves and others.

This message can serve as an additional reference in the personal profile or be used separately. Thinking of the purpose of the profile, I would use this information in another forum to ensure I didn't take away from the purpose of my study. However, because of the purpose of providing you with an example, I'll quickly summarize the decisions and consequences of the five men:

1. Solomon's disobedience brought adversaries and caused his son to lose almost the entire kingdom of Israel.

2. Rehoboam's decision to place a more substantial burden on his people cost him the ability to rule over the twelve tribes of Israel.

3. Jeroboam's fear caused him to create false gods and a religious system that led the ten tribes of Israel into sin.

4. The old prophet's lie led a man into sin and disobedience, causing his death.

5. The man of God's disobedience caused him to lose his own life.

CONCLUSION

I pray the information I've presented in *The Bible Study Blueprint* will help you study the Bible with greater clarity, understanding, and purpose. These tools, resources, and study methods have guided me for over twenty years, and now, I've passed them to you. Take this baton of information and run with diligence and patience to complete your race in Christ Jesus.

If you're ready to put what you've learned into practice, please review my study guide on discipleship, *Living for the Kingdom: Teaching What Jesus Taught.* This study guide provides 115 lessons on what Jesus taught His disciples in fulfillment of His Great Commission in Matthew 28:18–20. Go to the link provided in the footnotes to download a free PDF, or purchase a hardcopy or e-book.[97]

---

97 https://www.spiritualcombatants.com/books/.

GLOSSARY

Passage Study

City View

A review of Bible chapters surrounding a source scripture within the same book of the Bible.

Corresponding Scripture

A scripture of a similar topic or event.

Historical Context

Identifies a source scripture's intended message to its original audience.

Passage Study

A study that reviews biblical passages to understand its historical and personal context.

Personal Context

Derived from the historical context, personal context represents life lessons for personal edification.

Source Scripture

A scripture identified as the subject of a particular Bible study or review.

State View

A review of biblical books surrounding a source scripture.

Street View

A review of the verses surrounding a source scripture within the same chapter.

Word Study

External Topic Search
A topic search that uses pre-populated biblical references, such as a concordance or dictionary.

Internal Topic Search
A topic search that occurs without the help of a pre-populated biblical reference.

Topic Search
A study method that researches scriptures of a specific subject or topic in the Bible. There are two types of topic searches: internal and external.

Word Search
Examination of a specific word in the Bible for greater understanding or clarity.

Outline Study

Detailed Outline
An outline that adds supporting information to a simple outline.

Point Outline
An outline that identifies a specific subject or theme found in a source scripture.

Simple Outline
An outline that provides main ideas from a source scripture in a concise format.

Personal Profile Study

Personal Profile Study
A study that highlights specific individuals from selected source scriptures. They often provide

historical background information or identify specific life lessons or principles.

(com)mission

PUBLISHING

www.commissionpubs.com
info@commissionpubs.com

www.ingramcontent.com/pod-product-compliance
Lightning Source LLC
Chambersburg PA
CBHW071504070426
42452CB00041B/2287